Capricorn, Venus Descendant

Other Poetry Books by Michael Joyce

Light in Its Common Place
A Hagiography of Heaven and Vicinity
Biennial: Poems
Paris Views

Capricorn, Venus Descendant
50 Poems of Pandemos, Karkinos, & Eros

Michael Joyce

Broadstone

Copyright © 2022 by Michael Joyce

Library of Congress Control Number 2022934123
ISBN 978-1-956782-08-0

Design & Typesetting by Larry W. Moore
Cover photograph by the author

Broadstone Books
An Imprint of
Broadstone Media LLC
418 Ann Street
Frankfort, KY 40601-1929
BroadstoneBooks.com

For Larry Moore,
a gentleman and gentle man, who at the end of my writing life became "my publisher"
in a way any poet longs for and few are blessed to find. I am enriched by his dignity, his vision,
his love for all kinds of poetry (and bourbon), and most of all his abiding friendship.
Like his fellow Kentuckian, Wendell Berry, Larry "is always assured of the imaginative
sufficiency of the parish" and I'm happy he has taken me into his one.

Beyond that, this book so much makes manifest the "she," the figure of light, my life,
my partner in "building the second body, the vow, and working in the wonders,"
that its, and my, dedication to her is, I hope, transparent if not superfluous.
Ours is a dedication we know is eternal.

Finally, grateful thanks to my once Vassar colleagues and poets
in whose company I learned what it meant to be one
and whose generous comments grace this book's cover.

Contents

1.	Blankets	3
2.	Robe	4
3.	Frieze	5
4.	Pond	6
5.	Feet	7
6.	Abrasion	8
7.	Bowls	9
8.	Estuary	10
9.	Apotheosis	11
10.	Polar	12
11.	Tiger	13
12.	Birthday	14
13.	Sleep	15
14.	Philosophische	16
15.	Wow	17
16.	Forgot	18
17.	Waltz	19
18.	Art	20
19.	Ice	21
20.	Men	22
21.	He	23
22.	Leaf	24
23.	Honeysuckle	25
24.	Reticulate	26
25.	Mirth	27
26.	Passion	28
27.	Fell	29
28.	Afloat	30
29.	Swans	31
30.	Bend	32
31.	Serpentine	33
32.	Segments	34
33.	Träume	35
34.	It	36
35.	Gaze	37
36.	Limp	38

37.	Flame	39
38.	Laughter	40
39.	Ceremony	41
40.	Awake	42
41.	Garland	43
42.	Amabile	44
43.	Nostos	45
44.	Sound	46
45.	Liminal	47
46.	Nature	48
47.	Commedia	49
48.	Riverine	50
49.	Summa	51
50.	Sea	52

El amor supo entonces que se llamaba amor.
—Pablo Neruda, "Soneto LXXIII"

BLANKETS

The sweet burrowing beneath, embrace
of distant wave translated to mere thrum
down among tropic flats where seeming
weightless, the ray, all muscle and tendon,
swims, silken billowing become his palm's
steady pressure along the flank and buttock,
the nights of becoming wrapped in rapt
thrashing gone into something gentler,
fog of exhalation settling over the river,
rising, then sailing off beneath the sun,
nocturnal choreography embossed there,
veins of pulp couched onto the damp felt.

Robe

Bed warm body warm as the first blow lifted off
the shearer's clippers to broad hand and basket,
blast of lanolin exhales from the nakedness left
there, ewe's scent, your scent upon the disclosing
fingers which just as quickly close the soft ties
making an absent-minded allusion to the biblical
maiden at the well. So enrobed comes presently,
pleasantly, to mind a deeper nakedness at hand
a creaturely comprehension beyond catalogue
or enclosure, untethered lambling running off.

Frieze

Capricorn, venus descendant, limbs like a
Fawn's delicate pirouette or the surveyor's
Tripod unfolding, en pointe precisely for
This moment bathed in the blue nightlight
Swallow's origami emerging below the cove
Of the moon as seen from within herself
Given now to the one gifted with this calm
Pale wave enfolded now into pure volume

Pond

Seen in passing along the backroad to the studio
its moods multiple: troubled, serene, impassive;
colors intervals of tourmaline, eye unblinking
tambour de l'eau, low tone of the secret name
for the seam between light and movement
surface quivering beneath an unseen breeze,
timpanist's palm calming the trembling skin
that keeps the sky and waters in equilibrium
along the horizon where the low hills between
waist, rump, and flank converge for the sleeper
plucked from reverie hearing her whispering.

Feet

Bare, white beneath black Chinese trousers, porcelain
despite a birdlike armature belying high-fire origin,
soft as a dove within one's hands, yet with age betray
her, who herself climbed barefoot up upon a limb deep
in childhood woods to occupy herself with reading
among white-throated sparrows and cedar waxwings.
As a woman they wandered and learned things, some
secret and erotic in the sense of what makes a being
take on the form of itself, swelling sometimes, other
times staying placid as a nestling awaiting feeding.

Abrasion

Its verb not the past tense of being a bride
though this flowering, burning now beneath
the linen-wrapped ice feels a tiresome, tired,
insult, a litany of clichés of aging: cheeky jest,
strawberry colored, walked into... Accident
nothingness given form, how the body fails us
but never fails to be itself, her profile he says
classical, worthy of a Greek vase, etcetera, yet
does vault the steps on gimp knee, orangutan,
his well-meaning embrace meant to be what
love is ever even under present circumstance

Bowls

Holds an egg in her hand, two of them
juggles, fondles, smooths the scraps
of feathery paper wet with the paste
forms it into a container for emptiness
feels the concavity beneath her palm
the chick, naked and engorged, arise
and, tipsy, set off across the slippery
surface, O the wonders of men, she
thinks, are their vulnerabilities, their
qualities also, which she lists in gold
calligraphy upon each nested rim:
Prosper, Sage or Merit, Jake or Will,
it's all one, a wonder the sky holds

Estuary

There where the sea sleeps she seeks
to press against its flow, still point,
the infant she never nursed nestles
against her breast, conch's single
muscle latent in her lapsing grasp
gleams, like a lost dream, expanse
of the strand, damp sand a cushion
underfoot, the horizon within reach,
each breath the tide's distant message
awake turns to sleep, breathing deep
decapod calligraphy etched and then
erased as the creatures ease back in
where the waters, too, now exhale
lips met at the salt point now part

Apotheosis

Rod become snake becomes sparrow,
the bird depicted, tamed, nesting midst
catkins and acorns on the reverse of
the nymph's hand that languorously
traces the still-warm percale there
where the knee pressed against her,
she and fledgling unstirring, reverie
and memory intermix, milk or silk,
thread of lapis folded into titanium
or the way the snow becomes the hill

Polar

In the last dark hour, when sleep won't come
and dreams won't stop, this recurrent one, twin
bowls— a chocolate "hay" of pretzels and shreds
of white nutmeats, the other some savory sileage—
will not come to pass. Passing dish a quaint phrase
from the age of noir novels or housewife magazines.
"Did you—?" her, wise, ex used to ask. To go or
come. The woman out alone upon the enjambment
of jagged ice climbing up from the cabin outside
Manistee that winter not caring, without care—not
careless but carefree— used to run in place beside
the empty bed to warm herself enough to get in.
What solitary hermit, rifle or binoculars in hand
used to spy upon her there, blue parka against
the white, not a bear, nor bare as a matter of fact
except in his awe-filled, awful dreams, and think
maybe a fellow might could get into his truck
and go over and stand there, and how is he any
different at this instant than the half-erect dreamer,
neither one worthy nor, anymore, able to go there.

Tiger

What she recalls best from when they led her backstage
at Cirque d'Hiver as someone hunted up the gift affiche
was neither the robed aerialist's sisterly nod nor the weary
smile of the off-duty Monsieur Loyal but the pure force
of the beast in the wagon, energy uncontainable, ripple of
storm surge along the barrier island, sandy clump of paws
momentarily placid, claws retracting as the machiniste left
to load a cart of sequin décor for the next act. Languid eye,
its hues unsurprisingly those of the eponymous gemstones,
hardly taking her in, yet still thrilling. She's made a study
of lover's hands, one steady, another broad, one searching;
other appendages too, of course, albeit curatorial: this one's
tensile strength, the other's length, curve, that one's girth,
none the allure of its abated menace, pearl of its dew claw.

BIRTHDAY

Thinks he's making fun of her when he says she's sexy,
sharpening knives, standing at the counter looking out
at the river that the singer says she'd skate away on if
she had one, the stone, a wheel, now years older than
the half century her youngest son turned yesterday, its
angle just right, the knives rocking back and forth in
its cradle, hurt and anger he says he feels a signature
she knows too well, now three quarters the span since
the gadget came into her possession. Slowly rocking
as the pot boils over within him, yesterday he wanted
her to say how she felt then, the pain and isolation all
she could think of, today thinks to imagine her there
in that other kitchen, mimes how she would've danced
to "California." Men know nothing he knows as well
as she does the goat dance of the fellow who gave her
her smile back then or was that someone in a song?

Sleep

From age eighteen she's known to release
what has to leave, not her, but this abode of
glory and sadness, felt the compact creature,
still gilled, swim off into the firmament and,
miraculously, take flight, hesitant a moment
as if light itself, then settle midst the bright
host occupying foggy hills and backwater,
mesa and arroyo, radiant skim of pooling
bioforms that give shape, for good or ill, to
dreamscapes from which polliwogs crawl.
Saints or monsters, lovers or specters, she
felt—with fingers, on her forearms—years
before the morning, however you spell it,
began to foreshorten into seasons and pass.

Philosophische

She asks him to locate the sublime
in their house, infinity in a shadow,
unbearable canyon of awe where?
Wanton alp of mountain in a breast
he suggests, bare foot arched white
beneath the red bathrobe, raku vase
sitting just so on the narrow shelves
of wundercammerlich boxes. Are
you do you think more like Joseph
Cornell or Robert Motherwell? her
follow-up. Night games don't take
passion's place but augment and
annotate it, the philosopher's son
likes the smell of onions, she says,
though he doesn't like to eat them,
speaking of the past in the present

Wow

Was all, truly, she could say when he offered that her sex
was like the Holy Ghost, warmth and exhalation, or some
such English class stuff—Donne, Jonson, To His Mistress
and all that, or later, on her own, Henry Miller to Anaïs—
a girl could swoon to, she supposed, but she was used to
(used on reflection being the right verb) disproportionate
adoration, as when the test pilots swooped her up upon
the bar to strut those legs as at first the others whooped
but then swallowed their undue enthusiasm as another
gently set her down, no one, not she either, saying they
were sorry. Sorrow came with her dearest, disconsolate
sailor fiancée back from untimely burying his sister,
clasped together without protection, none possible then
nor consolation. Only that once and instantly pregnant,
sudden become a woman used to shared sorrow and
love, of course, really love, learned not from books or
poetic whispers but being there as her own life went on.

Forgot

It's as if his inventory of needs, hurts, and fears
were clipped into fortune cookie strips, slipped
into vintage glass medicine bottles dug up from
the yard, sealed, and set adrift into an eddy to
swirl. That complicated. In the current the glass
harmonium tinkles, clangs, and moans by turns,
meanwhile the wind howls, she's in the midst
of her own blizzard of doubt, what's to be done
unknown, say it breaks her heart, for a start,
suggest a waltz, he'd rather hypotheticals. Say,
he says, you'd been away for days and I forgot
to come to the airport. I'd take a taxi she offers,
bring my own bags in, come in and kiss you
say I've missed you, or is there something else
I'm missing, far from the shore, a maelstrom?

Waltz

Their waltz, that night, to the Sarabande of Bach's
Cello Suite #1 he proposes as literally intercourse;
maybe literarily she supposes, though frankly has
her doubts. There he goes again she thinks, sweet
old steer, yet when he recalls long-ago tangoists
seen along the colonnades at Place des Vosges, she
stops holding him to such rigid definition, the knee
scissoring insistence against the thigh in the paso
belongs to whom? Lost in the loose quebrada they
pivot as one in their media luna. And when he says
a crystal stream rises from beneath the low notes,
its dark current now a calming, gentle resonance
she waltzes the flow, presses their breasts to each.

Art

In her, not what it's thought, or thought itself, in her in
every sense, whether of thought or art, eros given form
together or apart, how effortlessly she folds and flattens
the foil on which the scarlet bowls will cure, the pencil
tracing their hands as if they themselves were doing it,
a grace that escapes language, not volition but condition,
open to what comes within its span, face in the night,
pale legs enfolding, center, cause to enter some as yet
ungestated form, her gestures sure as those of the goddess
in the Egyptian story who made of herself a bird to search
her consort's limbs and members strewn like chum upon
dark waters, then, by her art, to piece and resurrect him
awakening him to husband the birth of the falcon god
making of his right eye the sun, and his left the moon.

Ice

Reads her what she wrote of slurry and frazil and says
it is beautiful. Is it? she replies and they both know
the futility of having a past you cannot walk out upon
or a fresh word for what it is when you have it. Beauty
full he says his father pronounced it and she likes that
better. Than what? The slurry—"fields of ice curds"
as she had it, a surface at once less capricious or angry,
neither flurry nor fury, for a once young wife having
in her middle years sprung herself from what she did
not want to leave as much as had outgrown, moan of
the winds that, in her words, forced it shoreward and
made of it what Wiki calls snow "partially melted,
refrozen and compacted" a place to walk away upon
to nowhere, from no one, but toward whatever self
it was who echoed the moaning deep in its becoming.

Men

Suddenly she shares a memory of learning to skate upon a flooded field at her husband's sister's farm after the birth of their son. Something she wanted to do for herself, the family they had wanted done, widening circles begun without yet really knowing how far she would circle. She had to see in a way that phrase belies. Really had to, with her eyes as they say, who are always saying something. Men proclaim the free flow of freedom as a rule, when for her free is to know patterns before rhythms enter into the limbs, it's what frustrates watching the Tai Chi master on DVD together with him, happily flailing arms in circles, both of these men while she tries to take it in, one husband long ago skating off, this one now here just as long, disk spinning in the darkness of the machine, mastery not really impressed upon the silver rink within but rather in the air before her where she sees it.

HE

In his reveries, he says, he thinks his real heart
a hart, the kind the ladies carry in the tapestries.
In this initial confusion of the words and beasts
she's not sure she heard him right, hesitant since
grade school and the nuns as to which are homo-
nyms and which the homophones. No matter
she supposes, cloistered here with a mad monk
who thinks by this meditation to lower the sys-,
or is it the dias-tolic, or both, by telling it not to
tremble, tiny, tan creature more like a freckled
whippet, bald and soft, first stirring then calm
beneath the lady's devout and searching touch,
garden serene and ordered around them each.

Leaf

A "profound despair" took the form of a leaf,
neither emerald nor sage, ovoid, pointed, slim
in a plastic box a stick pin might've come in,
top transparent, dark foam beneath. A troubled
vision he bestows upon her the morning after
she's thought to help him through whatever
it was he had said had come over him. Surely
not this clear, comic, coffin lid; raft in which
apparition drifts and swirls in listless currents
and where, like chimeras, floats and disappears.
What is she to do with such a daft thing, save
snap the lid and trace a finger along its veins,
feeling the surface of dreams gone astray.

Honeysuckle

She and her sisters swarmed it like hummingbirds
she recalls when he describes the taste rising from
between. Nectar and sugary stamen, a word that
even then held a forbidden echo of what was to
come, curl of flower against the virgin tongue,
buzz of bees vying with the vibratory thrum
a delicious premonition of yet unknown aching
mid her loins, skin flushed, legs scratched, whole
wood humming a melody she'd remember after.

Reticulate

In the mixed season when the black limbs threaten
to give themselves back to greening, the near cove
covered over with a scud of little boats, he's afloat
also, latterly rigged with red rubber tubing, a tug
now, the tailored diaper like a codpiece, she finds
him somehow sexy and so he does also, they waltz
erect and supine allonged, it seems little more can
happen to them, but also that it shall, life scrawls
upon them, limb by limb, apparatus by appendage,
and they augment, they augment, splayed fingers
fanned into serviceable caress, they cling and span

Mirth

The tristesse which came over her as they held
she termed an existential moment thus he knew
unfathomable, so when she laughed helplessly
he joined in, swimmers adrift in a counterflow,
raucous current carrying eddy and them each
like a raft slowly upstream, buoyant and lazy
above the dark waters, vortices of unutterable
sadness, dim shoals encrusted with dark pearls,
sunk now in the vague witness of memories,
roil sifting itself into what passes for clarity,
the castaways reach for each other, vagrant,
deep in a last embrace, laughter echoing.

Passion

He thought she meant the night when she asked
would it take faith to believe a crocus in bloom,
of course, she meant in daylight where he often
spied her gazing. They were talking of divinity
before bed at her insistence after he showed her
the videos of the two young women in ek-stasis
preaching the passion of Jesus in a way she felt
unformed albeit compelling enough. They lay
tired from drinking the nightcap of Chartreuse
and Maraschino called the Last Word, caught
in the good news of their own sort, resurrection
ahead of them, dream of a long arising passed
into the past, easy in the company of each other.
Earlier she'd held up a small, perfectly formed
potato chip like a host, asking without irony
why it was that these tasted better than most.

Fell

Elegant as a fainting sylph or a scarf dropped
by a girl heading somewhere, why then this his
hysteria seeing her crumple there in the garden,
thinking her dead as the heroine in a stage play.
We will come to an end, she thinks, maybe even
drop, yet to comfort him—him— insists she'll
never die, though they each know that's a thing
only he can accomplish for himself. It's still so
next morning, she calm in symmetrical repose
pale as a sun-whitened shell, he the pearl diver
going deep, going down, spreading the grasses
seeking the light at the center as if it fell there.

Afloat

Each time setting out now toward open water,
he falters, clings, asks her to hold him there
in bodyless repose, limpet cowering below
the white umbrella of its calcified star neath
a dark sea. Despite his foothold, floating lost,
limbless, limping even upon the shore of her,
so sure elsewise, wide horizon toward which
he means to swim but loses all his erstwhile
buoyancy. When sudden in the shadow swell
its dark surface mirrors another sea aglow,
the upended apogee of another sky, her light
above them both, shining arc, steadfast boat.

Swans

The swans along the reservoir and wetlands beyond the highway as she drives do not glide but nest in shallows illuminated by their radiant whiteness. So too with him. She drops him off outside the hospital and watches him go in. Time passes in the shadows where she parks and reads. He comes out a new creature, though still himself, not ashen as others nor raw wet as a cygnet, yet chastened by the rays that chase what the pills cannot reach. Snatching him to her nest she preens him like a new hatched cob, after which she turns toward home and bed.

Bend

He likes to see her do what she does he says,
read the Times, say, in the old way, bent, intent
studious in eyeglasses. Likes to see her bend
in fact, not in the way of obsequiousness, god
forbid, or submission, but easy as seagrasses,
which, even windlashed, have an upright grace.
Not that he's without lasciviousness to be sure
who knows her curves even through trousers,
hers or his, theirs is a family of saltimbanques,
clownishly in love with what gives way, gives
ways to imagine entering into such complication

Serpentine

Caught in his own cleverness she reminds him when he forgets
what he'd offered as something of a riddle for the present rapture,
i.e., he: "One of us came and she was me," which, caught up not
in its gender but his syntax, she'd supposed he thought alchemical,
non-binary, or whatever, an Adam in a swoon naming creatures
for whom the turn taking of such sequential hermaphroditism was,
pardon the common place, second nature, fish, snails, or flowers,
say cobra lily a/k/a jack-in-the-pulpit, young bud turning labile
one after another over a lifetime, too damn many words for what's
something everybody knows without all the Latinate lace, erect
central spadix rising from a spathe, etc., sighs: who I am you are.

Segments

Splitting the clementine into what he insisted were segments rather than the sections she called them, she thinks they will miss these interludes, pastel spectrum of pale spring along the long corridor of highway there and back, a day, a week, a life of measures, he afterward rooting in the plastic sack for these pillows of plump halfmoons orange as day's end, white sap that used to signal some climactic given over to wheeze and clack of the tungsten leaves, rays that instead zap the desiccate taproot, now he emerges from there, to her, their sweet juice, and the road back

Träume

In her sleep he hears her almost soundlessly call his name,
more exhalation than utterance, glottal, forlorn, in reverie
covering him over with broad wing, white cloudlike thing,
its shadow sheltering him, filtering the rays as in the tale
from Delft* of the mother stork returning to her flaming nest
who "failing to lift her babies, allowed herself to be burned
along with those she was powerless to save." Loves him
that much that he tries to enter into her dream to tell her not
to cry out, not to flutter so against the flames that consume,
but ashen finds himself there briefly lost in a white room
until, breathless, washed, she emerges from the surf to see
the great ship sailing off, birds circling in its dark trough.

*"Consider the Stork" by Katherine Rundell, *LRB*, April 2021

It

It has left him a ruined isle just offshore of her, what "it" he
cannot say, nor why he takes the long way windward where
the sharp stones stand and not the lee strait across which she
reaches him on each side of the night, beach or strand it is
just words, he's less weary now, yet still cannot stand without
pushing awkwardly from the chair, feeling the bare wire there
where it attaches the awful thrill of its pain to burnished bone.
It is not the disease, which to a water woman has both its name
and spiny emblem, jeweled pincers like the cape's far reaches
out past Piney Point, crab shape of the pond she painted after
her other sailor took her inland all the way to Kansas. This one
she thinks was also a seaman in another life, the way he rocks
once up, as if on wooden legs, erect, a wreck, it is his to say.

Gaze

He makes a speech: You can only see what you see. You can't see anything wrong, you can't see yourself seeing. Your. Self. Any thing. Wrong, she thinks, thinks she sees him thinking this. Thinks. Sinks short of the sea she is supposed to see, or is she the leaf, and he the current? Or vice versa, she is glad he does not say that at least. His speech lapses to silence, he does not say he was looking at a girl in a yellow dress moving through a grove of elms, each more or less the same circumference, each illuminated equally by the single sun, yet separate, each itself, each splashed in light (she thinks he would have said caressed, as if light were liquid). He's stopped speaking now but holds her hands in his, as is the current by the river's banks, she thinks she sees him there, not moving along the bed, that's the river's to do for itself, we'll see what happens next, see what we

Limp

That the term could twice befall him they cannot have imagined,
of co- or incidental, to or in him, they expected only the latter,
all this logic tripped up by one muscle or another, he cries out
at the threshold of each, it's the one she cannot reach, pedestrian,
that weighs her down, resists guile or trancelike patience, cannot
be teased by silk or oil, beckoning finger or the palm's invocation,
lone witness of the drilling pain she remembers only thrice before,
she knows pain is metallic, its taste lingers, they ask you to push,
then not, then take it away unfairly before you've had a chance to
hold it, soothe it at your breast, feel the beating merge with yours.
He moves from room to room as if in rosined goatskin slippers
feeling for the wire cable, her own foot modeling the orchid's furl.

Flame

She spoke softly of all that it was not, not consumed by nor engulfed in it, not padre's shook foil, nor magus's flash paper, neither tongue's crimson glister nor gash of tropical fruit hanging above the two children who have suddenly appeared, whispering not of the mystery of it but its familiarity, a fire scrubbed clean of its own consummation, not post but past coition, yet so present that the eyes ache to touch its trembling leaf, hands a bowl to cup the flow of its gelatinous swim. It is as if night once again became twilight and then dawn in succession, time tumbling over itself like a girl turning cartwheels down along a grassy meadow toward a dark ravine where the light gathers into a stream, this parching flame liquid, satiated.

Laughter

Hearing him speak this word she brightened, thinking
this poem what he had, or would have, read, not such
an earnest unwinding of how yet another guru passed
power to a successor. His tale once done, she in turn
spun a freeform riff of what she'd read, of sweetgrass
braided into soft ropes and the underlying murmur
of trefoil and vetch which lends color to far-off hills
wherever the goddess lays her head. So now, too, he
follows suit, laughing in delight upon her lap, ear to
where the Bhaga unfolds, flower that gives its name
to the sacred, and life to every laughing thing, this
which the Tibetan lexicon illustrates with gilt lotus.

Ceremony

Has always been so, the deep scent along the river in the night,
skunks and deer watching soundlessly from the darkened lawns
and on the way back up the hill, intoxicated by the honeysuckle
seeing the moon there, a veiled half circle in the eastern sky,
golden light of a single bulb in the kitchen of the house where she sleeps,
nocturnal creatures going about their business, love among them,
the eventuality of leaving unspoken for now, the room spinning
as he slides into the bed, while below ancient sturgeon cruise
along the silt bottom of the channel off Diamond reef

Awake

Here on the eve of the first night in years they'll not
share this bed, neither know how to leave one another;
although in his family departing had its own slow reel,
each lining up as if at a wake, not coy about the echoes
of it nor speaking them aloud, father and mother left
finally to waltz in the hall with each refugee of love.
And so as he tries now to disguise his forlorn sobs,
she's suddenly uncertain of the choreography of how
to release this fugitive shadow and let sleep drift its
blue linen over them, but then he gently guides her
down, imprinting his lips upon the lacy caramel pistil
at the glowing center of the night blooming allium.

Garland

What comes to mind at this distance is a simple garland
of amaranth, two flowers strung with kitchen twine as if
by a magic child, a sorceress of sorts, simple red strand
dropped unseen midst the flurry of laughter and leaving
they witnessed two summers ago, a large Indian family
gathering up the picnic as the lapsing golden hour flared
upon brick-colored sand at Brackley Beach, whirlwind
of shook cloth, children circling, women gathering baskets
and lifting the brass teapot from its tripod, a half-dozen
handsome husbands flexing muscles, hauling coolers and
dismantling the crimson canopy carefully around where
Awa and Tata still lingered in their folding canvas chairs
watching the gold thread of Sandhya's hem disappear
above like threads of misty silver, already gaining tide
by which the garland would be snatched an hour after.

Amabile

Low sunlight illuminates the yellow day lilies on a twilight picnic for one, drinking water, watching the estuary before him languish gilt, she away, txting back and forth, southwest to northeast, imagining her there, her here, her head turning as in Stein's epigraph, "toward the falling water. Amiably." There must be a word for this longing, longing for the body amiably, ably allongée as they say, when they are together as they are at this distance, gone forth, fro, to, O how distant the distance now that there is no longer any way to be away. From the words that trace what comes and goes on screens nor from the remove of heft and surface, curve and velvet crease. On Facetime days before, he insisted he was by inclination hermetic, she laughed and said you mean hermitic, *eye* not *eee*, sealed away in your own way, of course. What is this river's course, he wonders now, devotee of crossroads, conjunctions, and all else conjugal, saltwater silting into sweet, silvery things spawning neath contrary flow of she, he, source and sea

Nostos

Doesn't fancy himself one of those gimpy gods or heroes, Ulysses or the soft-hearted centaur, Chiron, for instance, and it's not he who is returning, so why all the fancy lingo upon this occasion, arcanum poured into the porches of his ear by random Jesuits, whining here like Hamlet re: lecherous hebanon (who's she when he's at home?) as if the protagonist of his own story? Still does limp about the house, cane in one hand, Comet cleanser in another, used to seek to please his mother likewise, hoping when she came home she'd find solace reflected in the burnished porcelain. As a word for return, Nostos has a salt tang, sea-born mist, and distaff sadness about it, sail billowing up like Artemis's soaked dress lifted from her thigh by the storm receding as fast as it came. Would that her, now his, daughter's squall recede as swiftly, a blue she-crab scuttling into shallows, see her too returned to the house she never left, she too finding it as it had been and she within it although her mother has now gone home, Nostos never having had the neonate at her own breast, both now yearning for it, or if not, for a language equal to the way such women sustain.

Sound

More and more they'd made their own silence in ceremony well before her journey, yet differently now as they try to settle, rake a clear space in the noise as if among leaves fallen out of season, pale denuded limbs intertwine in a hollow beyond the highway, pressed close at the center of some newness, unmoving moving, the sounds thus difficult to parse, muffled thunder? he wonders; belated fireworks more likely she suggests, but then confides what comes to mind instead is how the low rumble of a plow awakens a sleeper early in the morning of a winter night, snow a static dapple stamped against the void, binaries inverted, sound and light no longer within each other nor without, seasons spent drifting toward uncertainty, climactic chord as what-comes-next and what-was intermix

Liminal

Seen so, back to him in the mid-length summer robe of kimono fabric, lit by the pool of yellow light from the bedside Arts and Crafts lamp, for him she evokes the creature à l'aube in the delicate etching by the Pennsylvania Parisian Mary Cassatt, of a woman bathing bent before mirror and basin, floral pitcher at her feet, its pattern a simple, floating-world wreath of red lilies—or are they scarlet iris?— each woman framed in an imaginal realm differently half-dressed, each coming into view as if through a mirror aslant. Once aware of him she turns, smiles and smooths the billow of the bedding, then together come downstairs to find a scrim of smoke along the twilit river, grisaille borne east by the jet stream from blazing forests a continent away. Over a lovers' supper of cold salmon and chou chinois, she conveys a story she has read about a renegade sect of insistently Roman-Catholic women whose own bishops consecrate their priests upon barges floating mid-river that churchmen believe form the natural borders between their dioceses.

Nature

The midday hollow echoes with an aggrieved shriek from an ornamental cock, hens all gone. A wolf trails the papery ribbon of a scat and nettle crusted tail rubbing it raw against a rotting stump. She and he set out to nap alone through this afternoon upon the queen bed in a vagrant space. She's been musing on the elegance of pecan paneling in a house she once built. "I can't," he says, and tries to choke his sobs in the white blanket of someone else's country house. A fly defies the silence and dies in ecstasy at the sweet scent of apples and shit. The weather is fairer and his despair more languid than the end of July deserves. The storm, when it comes, kettles in slow march cannonade. They spoon and press. Slow rocking turns to thrust and rut of some substance as the downpour subsides.

Commedia

She has had a dream of "everything," she explains, "Physics, waiting for trains, taking kids to practice." They lay awake in the interim between rain and flame in August at the beginning of a heat wave. The dream is full of characters and unfolds in various places, lastly a sort of theatre where a loud man a seat away has stolen her reading glasses and she awakes just as she leans over her lover to slap the thief. The lover, too, has been dreaming but he cannot say of what although he feels strangely pleased being there both with her in the dawn and on the railway platform, yet vaguely forlorn at neither having rescued her nor having been him there in the days when children had to be carted somewhere. Theirs has been a knot differently tied, scarlet cords of the P'anch'ang, its bud both open and closed at once, its instant where the butterfly alights on a lotus, pool vibrating across the whole of its surface, dream without end or beginning.

Riverine

On the bank of an unfamiliar rural river a half hour out of bed
too late for her to see the frog launch into the tallow and green
of the near shallows, they silently recall his prior evening's fall
into helpless syncope, gliding through successions of dim light
as if layers of gauze had slipped from him, or he through them,
unable to mouth any reply to her wise and patient questioning
yet grateful that she had taken him at his word and not denied
what had come as if a long-feared but not unrecognized event,
they watch the ripples widen and elide after the unheard splash.
One day, one and each, we will have to come down to the river,
he whispers then, after which she replies we will both jump in.

Summa

They have been counting things the sum of which they cannot calculate and— but not as a result— do not care about. It is of course too early for the characters of whatever comedy they think to appear in to say how their story ends, save that, pardon the pun, it involves a sort of salvation, a third body arising as flame does from a medicine bow, where the secret lies less in friction between the two bodies as it does in precise tenderness, the nest of tinder lifted from the depression where the stick twists against the hollow, sparking it into a brief existence that can only be sustained by folding it back within itself, fingers moving with insulated deftness, exploring the creases where heat settles into both things and creatures, only to be drawn out again, not as the weaver draws pattern from wool, but rather as forceps snatch a raku bowl from a kiln at the fire's peak.

Sea (with CG)

If one of us goes, she says, the other will launch into the ocean
of interstice, waters of the upper seas beneath which, still, this
river flows the course we've set for it, its tracery a marriage of
water and water, our sacred bed its source, bodies embossed
there like waves on sand. And the ocean above will know
by heart the shape of the snaking river, shifting stones, bits
of glass gracing its passage, a mosaic conjuring the third body.
When one of us goes, he says, the other will already be there
"where the two seas meet," our love a boundless estuary.

About the Author

Michael Joyce's sixteen books and several digital works span a career as novelist, poet, critic, theorist, digital literature pioneer, and multimedia artist. He lives along the Hudson River near Poughkeepsie where he is Professor Emeritus of English and Media Studies at Vassar College.

Even before the pandemic, he says he began to think of himself as "an everyday monk, reluctant to frame this stage of my life in terms of what I am going to do, or how I feel, or in any other way that has 'now' as an antecedent. That is, I resist thinking it an end or beginning of something, but rather as a continual folding and unfolding along a dimensionless surface, not something but not nothingness."

For more information, visit michaeljoyce.com.